Queen of the Campfire

Sweetly strumming on a banjo, crooning as a full moon rises over the mountains, a beautiful camper marries the 1930's theme of the open road with movie star glamour. The pattern for this 16" x 14" pillow is on page 30.

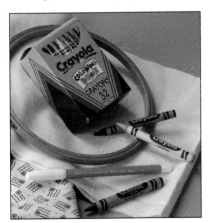

Teeter-totter

Nothing appeals more to mothers than healthy, smiling children busy at all sorts of games, especially outdoors. Naturally, children at play is a theme running through every type and style of needlework. Tinting makes for a bit of magic. Color adds movement and energy to a picture, giving it depth and letting it spring to life. You can almost see the teetertotter going up and down. The pattern for this 16" x 12" pillow is on page 31.

How-Tos for 'Tinting' with Crayons

Crayons Aren't Paints - Even though ironing softens the crayon, their hard nature means that some of the texture of the fabric and the strokes you make will show through - just like when you make a rubbing over a penny. Making your strokes in the same direction can be challenging in large areas, which is why projects with smaller individual areas of color are best suited to crayon tinting. **Tip:** Practice on extra muslin first.

Supplies - Muslin fabric, 24 colors of crayons (or more), embroidery floss, embroidery hoop, micron pen, needle

Crayon Hints - Besides being convenient, crayons come in beautiful colors and aren't intimidating. Simply color in the spaces to create the look you want.

Build Up Color, Edges In - Add layers of crayon color with the strokes going in one direction, or opposite directions for a darker effect. Start lightly - you can always add more. Shading built up from the edges inward helps model or add depth to the pieces, so that the tinted areas are not only colorful but 3 dimensional as well. You can even choose to leave an area completely open to give a strong highlight.

Use the Correct End - For filling in color, the blunt end of the crayon works best and it works even better if its hard edge is rounded off a little before you start. Keep the pointed end for details or adding a fine shaded line to edges.

Tip: Let the Fabric Do the Work - A shaded fabric (white on white or off white) adds depth to your shading. Larger designs are a little better than fine ones because they give more variety.

Days Off

Tinted pillows breezed into 1920's homes with a look as fresh as the first day of spring. Homemakers welcomed the convenience of tinted embroidery as enthusiastically as they welcomed other labor savers for the home.

Whimsical themes matching the light-hearted Jazz Age delighted adults and children. As homemakers sought every possible cheery distraction from the difficulties of the 1930's, carefree themes kept the blues away!

Bow - Wow Wickets

Many a funny bone must have been tickled by these bowsers, putting on country club airs! More sophisticated than a nursery project, the humorous nuances of a 16" x 14" pillow like this would have appealed to young women eager to decorate their rooms with their own handiwork, as well as to school girls embroidering for the first time. Pattern on page 42.

Horse & Carriage

As the Colonial craze entered its second decade, not a month went by when Colonial motifs weren't included in popular needlework magazines. Tinted pillows such as this were star attractions among an abundance of antimacassars and buffet scarves. In the high style of the mid 1930's, this 16" x 13" pillow is a wonderful example of the realism and detail favored in this trend. Pattern on page 43.

Sweet Dreams, Milady

The demure bonnet lady transformed the humblest room into "milady's chamber". This charmingly simple design asks only the easiest stitches to work her magic. Her style is typical of quilt blocks commonly found in the 1920's and 1930's, and she could easily be used for a cozy lap quilt or beautiful wall quilt. The embroidery pattern for this 11" square pillow is on page 34.

Spanish Dancer

Meet the Bonnet Lady's stylish Spanish cousin! Perfect for tango enthusiasts or those who dreamed of world travel, this elegant beauty demonstrates the late 1920's fascination with exotic themes. Many colors and a steady hand were required to develop her beautiful black shawl. A delicately tinted version would adapt this 16" round pillow to today's home decor and tinting methods. The embroidery pattern is on page 35.

Designer's Tip

Use ½" seam tape to bind some pillows or sew lace around the outer seams to trim other pillows.

Potholder Portraits

A thoroughly Modern Millie, this holder is more flapper than Colonial Miss. Holders were often shaped into figures far too pretty to use. Similar projects were created by applique, but bright tinted colors were crucial in the original designs. Patterns on pages 81-83.

Ladies in the Garden

Blossom Scape

The tinted background on this 18" x 14" pillow combines the silhouette trend of the 1920's and 1930's with the pastel palette of boudoir pillows. Enhanced by delicate colors on the hair, ribbon and blossom centers, the result is dreamy yet sophisticated. Pattern on page 33.

The Goose Girl

So much interest can be added with just a little color. This inspiring 15" square pillow shows just how far one color can go when combined with the classic 1920's touch of Black outlining. Easily recreated with a few touches of crayon, Delft Blue is another color option often seen with Dutch patterns from this era. The embroidery pattern is on page 32.

Fancy Ladies

With a hat brim as expressive as her beautiful face, tinted Bonnet Ladies were essential feminine furnishings in the late 1920's and 1930's. Flirtatious, mischievous, and enviably unruffled... each lady had a personality all her own.

As glamourous as movie and advertising poster art from this era, distinctive portrait style Bonnet Ladies like these were also called 'poster girls'.

Laundry Lady

Dainty lady for dainty laundry! A pretty bag for laundry was absolutely necessary in a feminine retreat filled with powder puffs and perfume bottles. Fancy lady linens matched the half-doll figures adorning powder puffs, clothes brushes and other finery. This charming 1930's laundry bag features a design that also appeared as part of a potholder set. The laundry bag shown is 17" x 28". The pattern is on page 79.

Roaring 20's

As decorative as any picture or plate, tinted novelty potholders became a trend in the mid 1920's. Distinctive holder frames usually integrated the shape of the holders as part of the design. Sometimes sets coordinated with novelty measuring sets, match strikers and string holders, all sold in the pages of the same needlework catalogs. Each of these ladies is centered on a 5" wide x 6" high piece of padded muslin trimmed with ½" Blue seam tape. The full size patterns begin on page 64.

Floral

Flowers, flowers everywhere - which one shall I pick! Grandmother had a lovely philosophy of home decoration - cover everything with beautiful flowers.

Morning Glories

Optimistic morning glory flowers were especially beloved during the Great Depression, but their popularity dates to the turn of the century. Here, colors and shapes reminiscent of 1940's block the corners of printed tablecloths, creating a pattern well suited to crayon tinting. Pattern on page 38.

Belle Bouquet

How striking! An ingenious 1930's design with small Black Running Stitches create shading that tricks the eye into mixing the color for the artist. This skillfully balanced design for a 16" square pillow can easily be tinted with crayons in a color scheme to match your own decor. Pattern on page 36.

Pink Ruffles Nosegay

Reminiscent of designs from the Rainbow Quilt Block Company, this 13" square nosegay pillow would also make a superb quilt. Lazy daisy wreaths and refined feminine style are typical 30's and 40's touches. Easily tinted, the bright blossoms can be colored to coordinate with any color scheme. Pattern on page 40.

Favorites

Gram's strategy ensured a generous supply of tinted floral motifs like these. Ideas on these pages suit any project or taste and the colors can be adapted to suit you.

Blossoms of Blue

Unmistakably Art Deco, this 16" square pillow updated 1930's Colonial style with background tinting. Embroidered shading enhances the breezy ribbon and blossoms with effective, yet simple details. The pattern is on page 37.

Fruit Basket

Pattern companies often updated popular patterns to keep them fresh, leading to the eclectic style found in this tablecloth corner pattern. Elaborate basket details recall early 1920's embroidery, but the fruit is tinted and embellished in 1940's colors. Pattern on page 41.

Nest Builders

Although this pattern is from the mid 1940's, its style and subject reach back to the turn of the century! Quite a lot of tinting has been used to decorate the corners of a tablecloth or a curtain. Soft colors like these can be crayon tinted very effectively. Redwork lovers can create a Victorian version by shading with just a little red. Pattern on page 39.

Americana & Native Nostalgia

Visions of happier times and places gave housewives a breather from the day's troubles during the Great Depression and WWII. When dreams of better days finally came true at the end of the war, such themes nourished America's enthusiasm for a happy, secure future.

In a way, tinted scenes of idyllic settings and native cultures recall the original purpose of tinting - to help embroiderers create a beautiful picture to adorn a pillow or a tablecloth.

Indian Maiden

An enchanting Indian Maiden, another version of the Bonnet lady, is a rare find from the late 1920's or early 1930's. Dreams of Indian life are captured in lovingly rendered details. Effective color and pattern make this 16" square pillow appear more complex to tint than it really is. Simple crayon coloring will recreate it, as long as a light hand is used to build the colors and skin tones. The embroidery pattern is on pages 26 and 27.

Señor & Señorita

Slowly swaying palm trees and carefree colors from south of the border appeared in the 1930's and 1940's. This couple is instantly recognizable to pattern collectors. During just a few years, the same artist created dozens of siesta motifs for pattern services and catalogs. Add as much color as you want to your 14" square pillow using crayons. The embroidery pattern is on page 29.

Trusty Burro

Donkey carts are an enduring motif from the Golden Age of California potteries. Linens to match lamps, planters and tableware featured sundrenched colors found in ceramics created by these influential companies. This motif is shown on a 12" wide dresser scarf. The pattern is on page 28.

Designer's Tip
Stitches are on page 97.

Popular Puppies

Wiggling, wagging wonderful puppies are poised to leap right into your heart. Just a few blushes of colorful tinting bring these very popular pillows to life. Often sophisticated enough for adults, simple stitching and effervescent personalities make them as rewarding to recreate as they were to embroider in the 1930's and 1940's.

Tortoise & Terriers

Tinting allowed designers to focus on capturing endearing expressions and details that tell a little story - it's plain these littermates are poised to make a reluctant new friend. The results are a heart-warming 14" square pillow from the early 1940's. The pattern is on page 45

Waiting...

Thanks to Fala, FDR's beloved companion, Scotties were a popular design in needlework novelties for over a decade. On this 17" x 14" pillow from the 1930's, impish Scotties are combined with the equally popular cottage theme. Can't you almost see their tails wagging? The pattern is on page 44.

Bowser's Big Band

From their swinging horns to their tapping toes, these pups are the top of the pops! Any Lindy-hopper from the late 1930's on would have treasured this charming 16" x 14" pillow, perfect for relaxing after 'cutting a rug'. Although simple to stitch, adorable details and artful tinting make this special pillow well worth recreating. The pattern is on page 46.

Plaid Pals
There's no mistaking these early 1930's pals, who mimic not only plaid but applique as well. Gingham, calico and plaid patterns frequently added texture and contrast to Depression Era embroidery designs, yet this tinted combination is rather rare. Pattern for the 15" square pillow is on page 49.

Close Quarters
Clearly this pillow depicts a very short lived truce! Airbrushed shading allowed artists to create many textures in one piece. Contrasting a smooth bow tie with fluffy fur, as seen on this 16" square pillow, was a common way to enhance the design of animal motifs. You can use the same idea by adding a real satin bow for a different yet easy variation. The pattern is on page 47.

Double Trouble
Surrounded by blossoms, this kitty and puppy were obviously raised to be lifelong pals. Designs like this one, combining large embroidered motifs with small tinted areas, emerged in the 1940's. Crayon can be used to tint this 19" x 15" pillow. The pattern is on page 48.

Pet Pals

An entire niche of novelty pillows grew out of the popularity of the "Gingham Dog & the Calico Cat" poem. Pairing the world's oldest odd couple led to pillows with as much personality as any teddy bear. Soon graduating from nursery to den, the pillows often told a mischievous tale that appealed to adults and children alike.

Crib Sheets

Three generations of young mothers tucked children underneath beautifully colored, bed-sized pictures which sometimes included matching pillows or tuck-in toys. Commercially tinted crib sheets offered large designs as delightful as those in any picture book.

Just Playing

Typically, crib sheets told a little story. This sweet 'tail of the dog' from the mid 1930's pairs adorable litter mates with running stitch outlining for a crib sheet that was easy to make and enjoy. With the addition of a matching pillow case, many crib sheets grew up with baby into a first childhood bedspread. This design could be used to decorate a pillow case or make a framed picture by reducing the size on a photocopier. The pattern is on pages 50-53.

Fun for Two

The mischievous shenanigans of these early 1940's puppy and kitty pals are meant to appeal as much to mother as to baby. Patterns for tuck-in toys which matched the sheet design were often available in the same catalogs, and these little figures can be made into soft toys by transferring the patterns individually and simply adding a seam allowance around the outer edges of the shape. The pattern is on pages 54-57.

All Stitch Diagrams are on page 97.

Time to Play

In the 1920's and 1930's, projects were often sold semi-finished with lace or ruffle trim. Mother might extend the life of a crib sheet to early childhood by adding her own ruffle. The pattern is on pages 62-65.

Bunny Go Round

Bunnies, balloons and bubbles were favorite 1940's and 1950's themes. Imagine this motif reduced to fit a little dress, playsuit, or even a birth announcement! The finishing details and style of this crib sheet suggest it was time-consuming to finish, but think again. Skillful design made the most of limited embroidery, allowing most crib sheets to be easily and quickly made. The pattern is on pages 58-61.

Bunny Pillow

Fairy themes rose to popularity in the 'teens, even appearing in reading primers. A coloring book or redwork design may have inspired this unusual piece. Showing the hallmarks of a home-tinted project, the naive style of this darling pillow suggests an ingenious mother created her own tinting pattern - just as we do today! The pattern is on page 25.

Baby Quilts

Kewpies, Dutch Babies, the Campbell Kids - adorable babies were as decorative as duckies or bunnies in the tinted nursery.

Following the trend for coloring book quilts, mother often made her own designs from traced coloring book pictures instead of buying commercially made blocks.

Embroidery styles in nursery quilts and crib sheets tended to follow the look of popular picture books, especially in images of babies themselves. Collectors can train their 'eye' by paying close attention to children's books from their favorite era.

Garden Cuties

Favorite picture book characters were among the earliest tinted novelties, later evolving into projects like this quilt for the nursery. Barely as big as a rose or daisy, these cuddly sprites might be Kewpies or just one of the many period Kewpie doll look-alikes that capitalized on Rose O'Neill's delightful illustrations. The soft colors lend themselves well to crayon tinting. Just a little pink in the cheeks will add a rosy glow. The quilt is made up of 5 white embroidered blocks combined with 4 pink plain blocks. Cut each block 12" x 10". Use a ¼" seam allowance and tie the corners of the blocks with ¼" pink satin ribbon if desired. Patterns are on pages 66-70.

Dutch Babies

Early Dutch motifs in redwork were among the first popular nursery themes. Their charm endured and Dutch children appear in nursery accessories until well into the 1940's. The distinctive blue associated with Dutch motifs made them particular favorites for tinting with just a few Yellow touches to brighten the designs. The pattern is on pages 76-78.

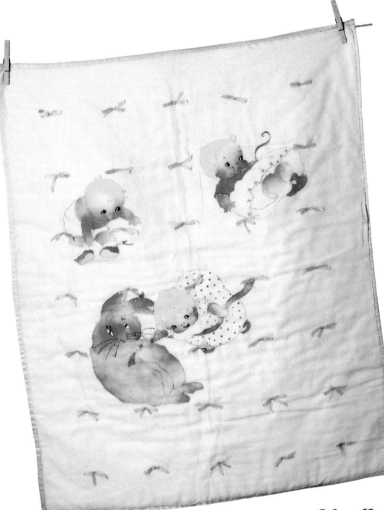

Potholders

Baby bonnet potholders are one of the most recognized themes of novelty embroidery. These cuddly characters developed in great variety during the 1940's. Wonderfully adaptable to pillows, pockets or even a tuck-in toy, just a little lace, crayon and thread will bring them to life for you. Pattern and instructions are on page 80.

Stitch Diagrams are on page 97.

Cloudkins

The large format of crib sheets encouraged designers to indulge their imagination and skill. Whimsical children's illustrations obviously inspired this especially charming example from the late 1920's or 30's. Batting added at home transformed this sheet into a warmer quilt. Any one of these babies would make an adorable tuck-in toy or could be separately embroidered for a series of nursery pictures. Patterns are on pages 72-75.

Children at Play

New mothers and babies were lovingly showered with embroidered accessories as a matter of course in the 1920's, 1930's and 1940's. Where would a young mother be without a place for messy bibs and onesies? In addition to designs like this beautiful Art Deco illustration, laundry bunnies, clowns and babies were also available. The pattern is on page 71.

1. Use a ¼" seam allowance throughout to assemble the quilt.

2. With right sides facing, sew an embroidered square to a 9" Pink sashing strip, add another embroidered square. Stitch another sashing strip and an embroidered square at the end. Repeat to make 4 rows. Press the seams open.

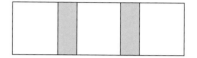

3. Alternate three 8" sashing strips with 2 Blue squares to make 3 rows. Press the seams open.

4. With right sides facing, sew the rows together as shown in the assembly diagram below. Press the seams toward the narrower rows.

5. With right sides facing, sew the 2 backing pieces together down the center long edge. Press the seam open.

6. Layer the backing, batting and the assembled top to form a sandwich. Baste the layers together.

7. Quilt as desired.

8. Remove the basting stitches. Trim the backing and batting even with the edges of the quilt top.

9. Bind the edges with the Blue strips, mitering the corners. Fold back ¼" along each long edge of each binding strip. Whip stitch the folded edge down the back of the quilt, placing it ¾" from the edges. Fold the binding strip to the front and whip stitch that folded edge in place to form a ¾" frame for the quilt.

Animal Quilt

FINISHED SIZE: 44" x 56"

MATERIALS:
- 44" wide, 100% cotton fabrics:
  2½ yards of White for design blocks and backing
  1½ yards Pink print for sashings and borders
  ⅛ yard Blue print for corner squares
  1½ yards of solid Blue for binding
- 48" x 60" piece of batting
- Assorted embroidery floss
- Assorted crayons
- White and Blue sewing thread

CUTTING:
- Cut twelve 8" x 9" White blocks.
- Cut 6 Blue print 4" squares.
- Cut 9 Pink print 4" x 8" sashing strips.
- Cut 8 Pink print 4" x 9" sashing strips.
- Cut 2 Pink print 4" x 45" side border strips.
- Cut 2 Pink print 4" x 36½" top and bottom border strips.
- Cut 2 White 24¼" x 60" pieces for the backing.
- Cut solid Blue 2" strips for binding.

DESIGN BLOCKS:
Transfer the designs on pages 19 - 24 to the White fabric squares. Embroider the designs. Follow the Basic-Tos on page 3 to tint each block as desired.

Animal Quilt

Quilt photo on page 18.
Instructions on page 18.
Enlarge patterns 118% to fit each
finished 7½" x 8½" square.

Animal Quilt

Quilt photo on page 18.
Instructions on page 18.
Enlarge patterns 118%
to fit each finished
7½" x 8½" square.

Animal Quilt

Quilt photo on page 18.
Instructions on page 18.
Enlarge patterns 118% to fit each
finished 7½" x 8½" square.

Animal Quilt

Quilt photo on page 18.
Instructions on page 18.
Enlarge patterns 118% to fit each
finished 7½" x 8½" square.

Animal Quilt

Quilt photo on page 18.
Instructions on page 18.
Enlarge patterns 118% to fit each
finished 7½" x 8½" square.

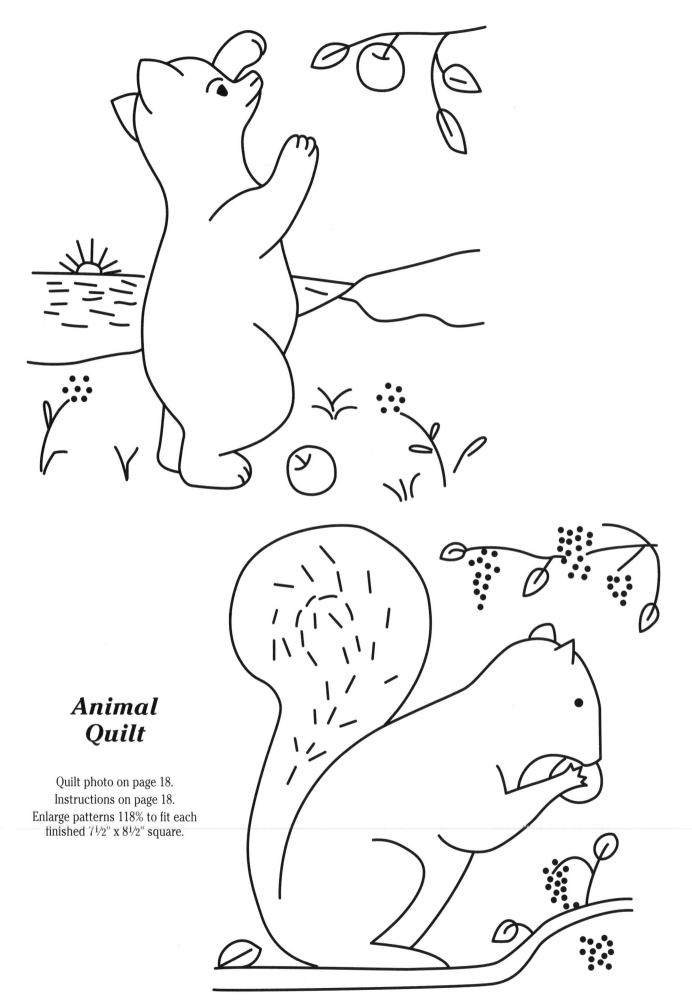

Animal Quilt

Quilt photo on page 18.
Instructions on page 18.
Enlarge patterns 118% to fit each
finished 7½" x 8½" square.

Bunny Pillow

Pillow photo on page 15.
The pillow shown measures 17" x 10".
Enlarge pattern 150% to measure 16" x 9".

Indian Maiden

Pillow photo on page 11.
The pillow shown measures
16" square.
Enlarge pattern 130% to
measure 14" wide.

Trusty Burro

Photo on page 11.
The dresser scarf shown
measures 12" across.
Enlarge pattern 120% to
measure about 9" high.

Señor & Señorita

Pillow photo on page 11.
The pillow shown measures 14" square. The edges are
bound with ½" Black seam tape.
Enlarge pattern 130% to measure 10" high.

The smell of pine, a wisp of smoke,
an owl calls from the wood.
I'd make a summer's camp my home
and wander if I could.

Queen of the Campfire

Pillow photo on page 3.
The pillow shown measures 13" x 11".
The edges are bound with ½" Red seam tape.
Enlarge pattern 150% to measure 13" x 11".

The pillow shown measures 13½" x 10½"square.
The edges are bound with ½" Red seam tape.
Enlarge pattern 140% to measure 13½" x 10¼".

Teeter-totter

Pillow photo on page 3.

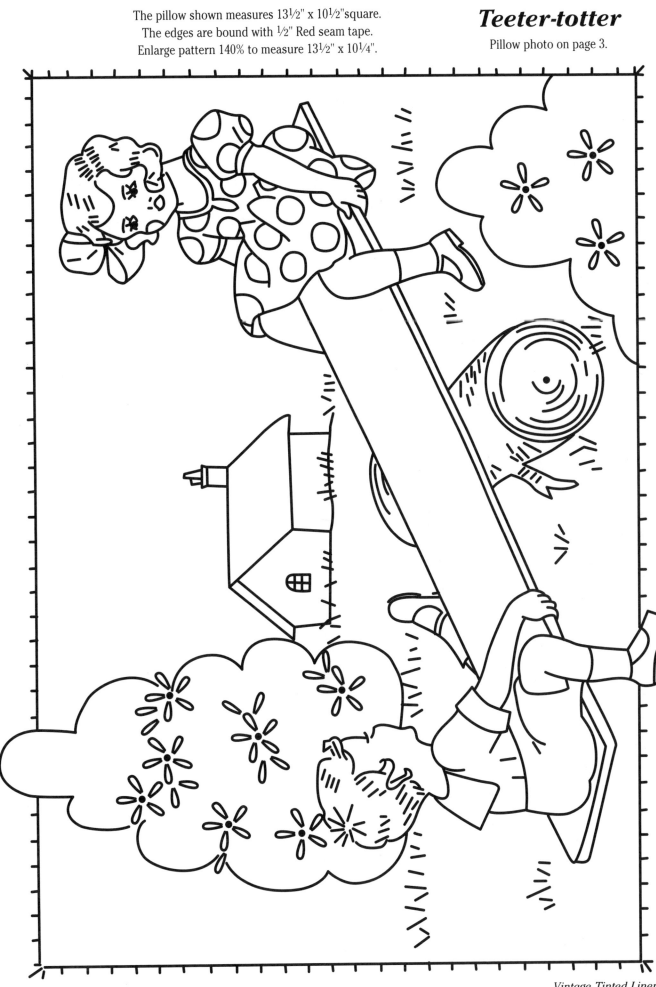

The Goose Girl

Pillow photo on page 6.
The pillow shown measures 15" square.
Enlarge pattern 120% to measure 14" square.

The pillow shown measures 18" x 14".
Enlarge pattern 170% to measure 16" wide.

Blossom Scape

Pillow photo on page 6.

What lady wouldn't wish to wear a bonnet with such flair.
It adds a touch of elegance to any style of hair.
Flowered, felt, straw or cloth, anything will do.
A favorite hat will warm her heart, no matter old or new.

Sweet Dreams, Milady

Pillow photo on page 5.
The pillow shown measures 11" square.
Pattern is shown at 100%.

Spanish Dancer Pillow

Photo on page 5.
The pillow shown measures
16" across
Enlarge pattern 140% to
measure about 11" wide.

A flower goes most anywhere,
On pillows, wall or in the hair.
A gift from God must surely be,
This bit of versatility!

Belle Bouquet

Pillow photo on page 8.
The pillow shown measures 16" square.
Enlarge pattern 160% to measure about 12" wide.

Blossoms of Blue

Pillow photo on page 9.
The pillow shown measures 16" square.
Enlarge pattern 170% to measure about 13" wide.

Morning Glories

Photo on page 8.
The project shown is a tablecloth with the pattern set
'on the point' at each corner.
Enlarge pattern 140% to measure 11" wide.

Nest Builders

Photo on page 9.
The project shown is a tablecloth with the pattern set
'on the point' at each corner.
Enlarge pattern 140% to measure about 13" wide.

Pink Ruffles Nosegay

Photo on page 8.
The pillow shown measures 13" square.
The pattern is set 'on the point'.
Enlarge pattern 140% to measure about 14" wide.

Fruit Basket

Photo on page 9.
The project shown is a tablecloth with the
pattern set 'on the point' at each corner.
Enlarge pattern 170% to measure 13" wide.

Bow-Wow Wickets

Pillow photo on page 4.

Enlarge pattern 150% to measure 15" wide.
The pillow shown measures 16" x 14".

Horse & Carriage

Pillow photo on page 4.
Enlarge pattern 125% to measure 12" wide.
The pillow shown measures 16" x 13".

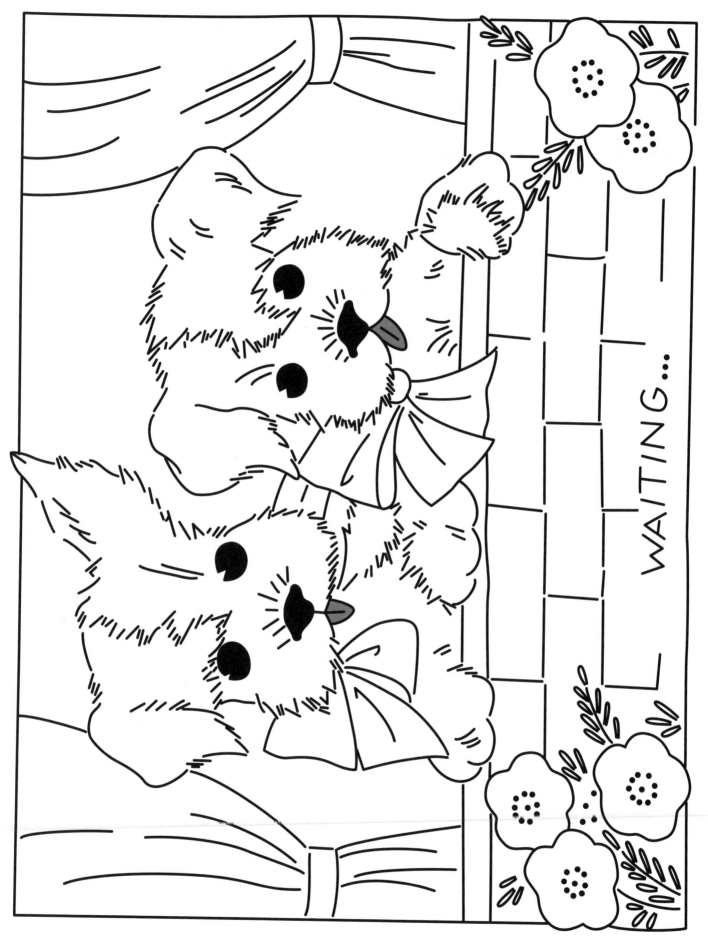

WAITING...

Waiting...
Pillow photo on page 12.

Enlarge pattern 125% to measure 9" high.
The pillow shown measures 17" x 14".

How hard it is to sit and wait,
to hear our master's call,
And see him coming up the path,
My, he does seem tall.

He makes our home and shelters us
from wind and rain and storm.
He take us up into his heart,
There keeps us safe and warm.

Tortoise & Terriers

Pillow photo on page 12.
The pillow shown measures 14" square.
Pattern is 100%, it measures about 8" high.

Look! A critter from a puddle?
Do you think he wants to cuddle?

Bowser's Big Band

Pillow photo on page 12.

The pillow shown measures 16" x 14".
Enlarge pattern 140% to measure 13" wide.

Pups and Kits, who could have guessed
Could be such special friends.
To romp and play, to share their home,
Together to the end.

Close Quarters

Pillow photo on page 13.
The pillow shown measures 16" square.
Enlarge pattern 180% to measure 13" high.

Double Trouble

Pillow photo on page 13.
The pillow shown measures 19" x 15".
Enlarge pattern 120% to measure about 14" wide.

"They'll never be friends,"
That's what they said.
But when opposites attract,
It's not all bad!

Plaid Pals

Photo on page 13.
The pillow shown measures 15" square.
Enlarge pattern 150% to measure 12" square.

Work, work, work,
Play, play, play.
What a way to spend
the day!

Just Playing

Crib sheet photo on page 14.

The crib sheet shown measures 32" x 47". Add a ¼"
seam allowance around all edges before cutting the
muslin. Center the pattern on the muslin. Add additional
flowers around the pattern as desired. Finish the
edges as desired.

Enlarge pattern 125% to measure about 22" wide.

Continued on page 52.

Just Playing
Continued from page 51.

Fun for Two

Crib Sheet photo on page 14.

The crib sheet shown measures 51" x 66". The center panel measures 28" x 41". Center the design on the center panel. Each side sashing measures 12" x 41". The top and the bottom sashings each measure 28" x 12". Each corner block measures 11" x 12".

Add a ¼" seam allowance around all edges before cutting the muslin. Press seams flat. Sew ⅝" decorative seam tape over each seam on both sides of the sheet. Finish edges with seam tape.

Enlarge pattern 110% to measure 20" wide.

Continued on page 56.

Fun for Two
Continued from page 55.

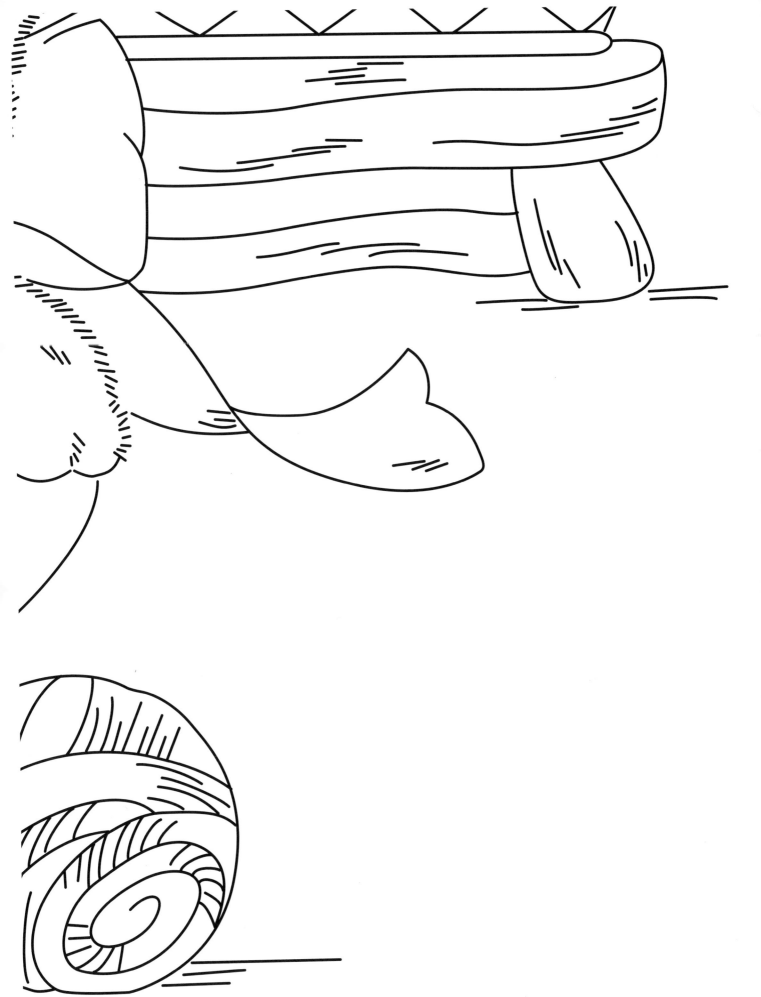

Bunny Go Round

Crib Sheet photo on page 15.

The crib sheet shown measures 32" x 47". Add a ¼" seam
allowance around all edges before cutting the muslin. Center
the design on the sheet. The Herringbone Stitch border around
the pattern measures 21" x 31". Finish edges as desired.

Enlarge pattern 105% to measure a little over 20" wide.

Continued on page 60.

Bunny Go Round

Continued from page 59.

Mary's lamb, circus clowns that
frolic in the ring,
Soldiers marching, kittens playing,
almost anything.

Time to Play

Crib Sheet photo on page 15.

The crib sheet shown measures
29" x 46". Add a ½" seam
allowance around all edges
before cutting the muslin.

Center the design on the sheet,
embroider and tint.

Fold back ¼" twice along each
edge to hem the sheet.

Enlarge pattern 125% to measure
about 20" wide.

Continued on page 64.

To make a ruffled coverlet, cut 2 Pink 9½" x 62" pieces of fabric.
Fold back ¼" twice along each long edge, stitch. Repeat to hem each
end of each ruffle. Overlap one long edge over the edge of the
embroidered sheet 1". Gather and stitch the ruffle in place along
each edge of the sheet. For the end ruffles, cut 2 Pink 9½" x 40"
pieces of fabric. Hem and stitch the end ruffles in place as before.

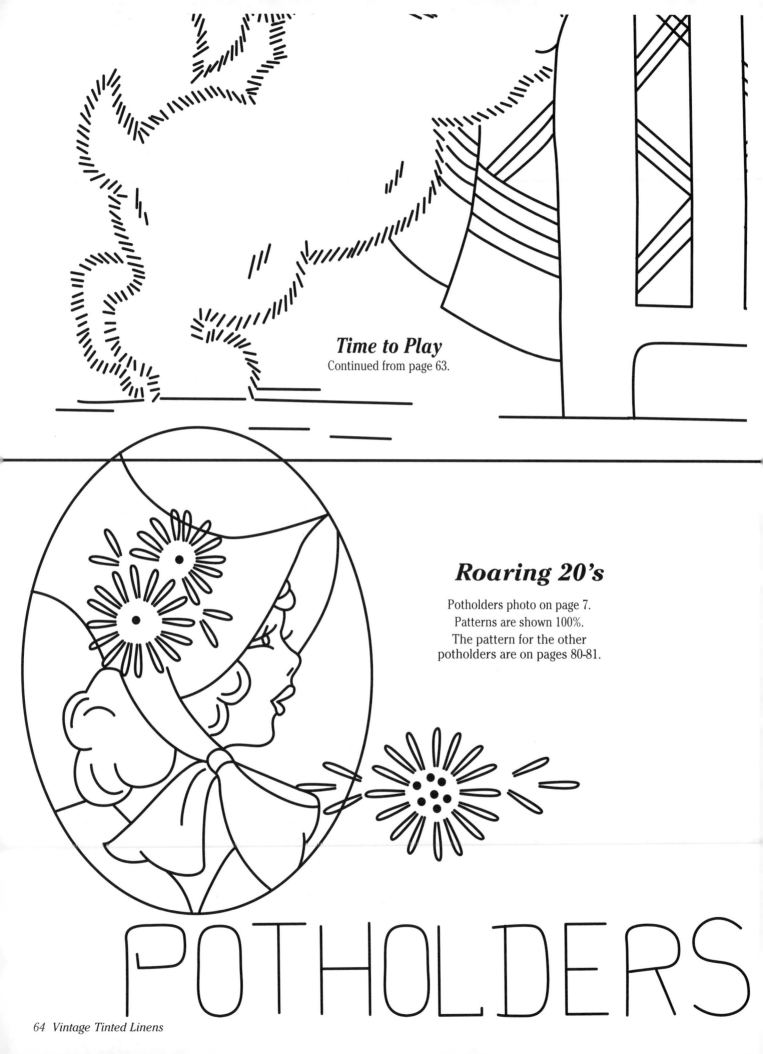

Time to Play

Continued from page 63.

Roaring 20's

Potholders photo on page 7.
Patterns are shown 100%.
The pattern for the other
potholders are on pages 80-81.

POTHOLDERS

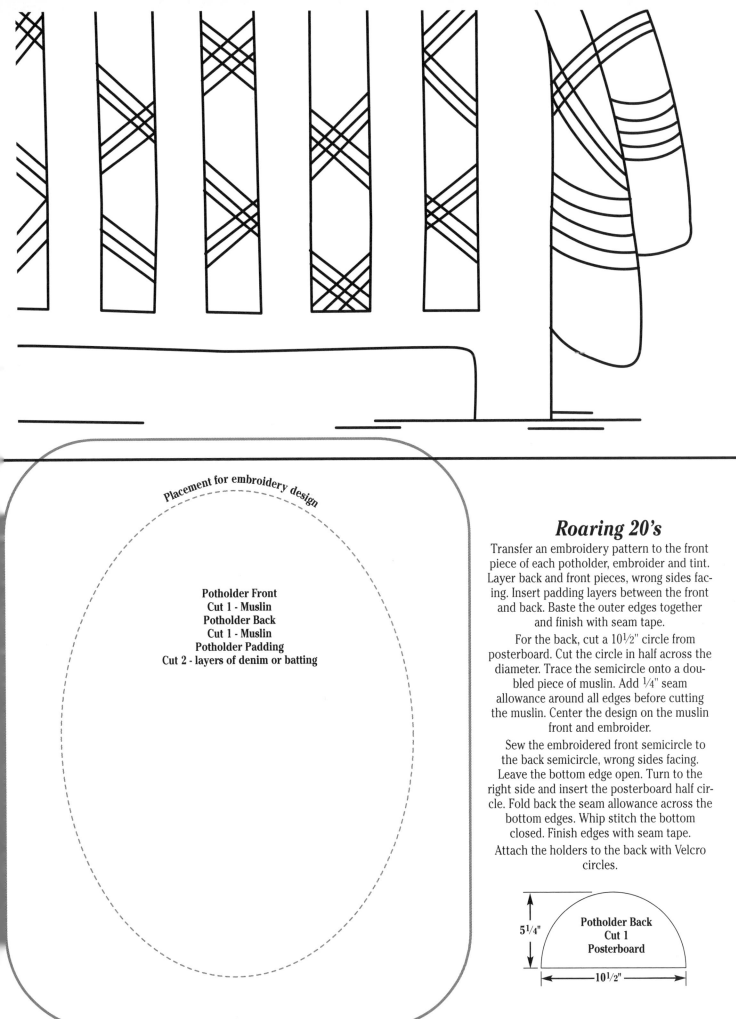

Placement for embroidery design

Potholder Front
Cut 1 - Muslin
Potholder Back
Cut 1 - Muslin
Potholder Padding
Cut 2 - layers of denim or batting

Roaring 20's

Transfer an embroidery pattern to the front piece of each potholder, embroider and tint. Layer back and front pieces, wrong sides facing. Insert padding layers between the front and back. Baste the outer edges together and finish with seam tape.

For the back, cut a 10½" circle from posterboard. Cut the circle in half across the diameter. Trace the semicircle onto a doubled piece of muslin. Add ¼" seam allowance around all edges before cutting the muslin. Center the design on the muslin front and embroider.

Sew the embroidered front semicircle to the back semicircle, wrong sides facing. Leave the bottom edge open. Turn to the right side and insert the posterboard half circle. Fold back the seam allowance across the bottom edges. Whip stitch the bottom closed. Finish edges with seam tape.

Attach the holders to the back with Velcro circles.

Potholder Back
Cut 1
Posterboard

5¼"

10½"

Garden Cuties

Quilt photo on page 16.
Patterns are shown 100%.

*Swaddle a sweet bundle of
joy and sing a lullaby.*

The finished quilt measures 28½" x 31½".

Cut 5 White 11½" x 10½" blocks. Center an embroidery pattern on the front piece of each White block, embroider and tint. • Cut 4 Pink 11½" x 10½" blocks. • Use ½" seam allowance throughout. Sew the embroidered and Pink blocks together in alternating rows as shown in the photo. • Cut one 29½" x 32½" Pink fabric backing. Cut one 28½" x 31½" piece of batting. Layer back and front pieces, wrong sides facing. Center batting between the front and back. Baste the layers together. • Fold under ½" along each outer edge of the quilt front and backing fabric. Secure the edges together with buttonhole stitches. • To quilt layers together, tie through all layers at the intersecting corners of the blocks with a 3" piece of ¼" wide Pink satin ribbon. • Remove basting stitches.

Garden Cuties
Continued from page 67.

A cover bright to grace the bed,
to make a young child glad,
Helps to brighten up the room
of any lass or lad.

Garden Cuties

Continued from page 69.

Children at Play

Laundry Bag photo on page 17.

The laundry bag shown measures 17" x 21" with a 7" slit on the center of the bag back. Add $\frac{1}{2}$" seam allowance around all edges before cutting the back and front muslin pieces. Finish the edges of the slit with seam tape.

Enlarge pattern 130% to measure a little more than 14" wide.

LAUNDRY

Cloudkins

Quilt photo on page 17.
Patterns are shown 100%.

The finished quilt measures 36" x 48".

Cut one 37" x 49" White fabric front. Transfer the embroidery patterns onto the front of the piece, referring to the photo for placement ideas. Embroider and tint the designs.

Cut one 37" x 49" piece of fabric for the backing.

Cut one 36" x 48" piece of batting. Layer back and front pieces, wrong sides facing. Center batting between the front and back. Baste the layers together.

To quilt layers together, tie through all layers of the quilt, using 3" pieces of $1/4$" wide Blue satin ribbon. Begin 6" below the top edge of the batting and 6" in from one side. Tie a row of 5 ribbons 6" apart. Tie subsequent rows 6" below the first one. Tie 7 rows.

Remove basting stitches. Fold under $1/2$" along each outer edge of the quilt front and backing fabric. Secure the edges together with buttonhole stitches.

Cuddle up in the quilt and enjoy a cup of tea to celebrate yourself for a few minutes.

Continued on page 74.

Such a gift is warmly met
and used night after night.
For what child wouldn't welcome this,
hug and hold it tight!

Cloudkins

Continued from page 73.

Dutch Babies

Quilt Photo on page 16.
The quilt shown measures 36" x 50" .
Enlarge pattern 160% to about 17" wide.

Continued on page 78.

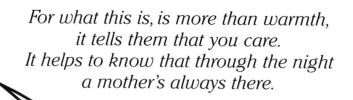

For what this is, is more than warmth,
it tells them that you care.
It helps to know that through the night
a mother's always there.

Cut two 17½" x 28" pieces of muslin. Shape the top to curve across a wooden clothes hanger. Transfer the design to the front piece, embroidery and tint. Cut an 11" slit down the top center of the front piece above the design. Finish the edges of the slit with ½" Red seam tape. Baste the outer edges of the front and back together, wrong sides facing. Finish the raw edges with seam tape.

Laundry Lady

Laundry Bag photo on page 7.
Enlarge pattern 180% to a little less than 14" wide.

Lace Placement

Potholder Front/Back
Cut 2 - Muslin

Baby Face

Potholder photo on page 17.
Pattern is shown 100%.

Cut 2 White fabric circles for the front and back. Transfer the design onto the center of the front piece, embroider and tint. Sew a $5\frac{1}{2}$" piece of $\frac{1}{2}$" lace across the top of the face as shown on the pattern.

For the ruffle, cut a $1\frac{1}{4}$" x 26" piece of Pink fabric. Fold back $\frac{1}{4}$" twice along one long edge of the strip, stitch. Using $\frac{1}{2}$" seam allowance, sew the short ends together to form a circle. Fold the seam allowances back twice and stitch to make a finished seam. Make running stitches along the other long edge of the ruffle $\frac{1}{4}$" inside the raw edges. Pin the ruffle seam onto the back circle of the potholder, aligning the raw edges of both pieces. Pull the running stitches to gather the ruffle evenly around the outer edges of the circle. Pin or baste the ruffle in place.

Layer the potholder front on top of the back/ruffle pieces, wrong sides facing. Sew the front to the back, leaving a $1\frac{1}{2}$" opening at the bottom. Turn pieces to the right side. Insert one or two $5\frac{5}{8}$" circles of batting into the potholder. Sew the opening closed. Make small randomly placed stitches through all layers to secure the batting layer in place.

Add 1/4" seam allowance around the outer edges of the design before cutting fabric

Roaring 20's

Continued from page 64.
Pattern is shown 100%.

A hot pad's such a clever gift,
To stitch up for a friend.
Flower, pup, or fair-haired gal,
Our pots they'll gladly tend.

Potholder Portraits

Potholder photos on pages 6 and 7.

Pattern is shown 100%.

Potholder Front/Back
Cut 2 - Muslin for each
(Add 1/4" seam allowance around the outer edges of
the design before cutting fabric.)
Potholder Padding
Cut 1 - Batting for each
(Cut batting just smaller than outer line of design.)

Continued on page 82.

Add ¼" seam allowance around the outer edges of the design before cutting fabric

Leave front and back open between marks.

Potholder Portraits

Continued from page 81.
Patterns are shown 100%.

Potholder Purse Front/Back
Cut 2 - Muslin
(Add ¼" seam allowance around the outer edges
of the design before cutting fabric.)
Potholder Padding
Cut 1 - Batting
(Cut batting just smaller than outer line of design.)

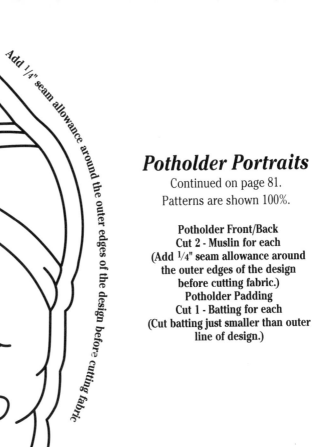

Potholder Portraits

Continued on page 81.
Patterns are shown 100%.

Potholder Front/Back
Cut 2 - Muslin for each
(Add ¼" seam allowance around
the outer edges of the design
before cutting fabric.)
Potholder Padding
Cut 1 - Batting for each
(Cut batting just smaller than outer
line of design.)

Add ¼" seam allowance around the outer edges of the design before cutting fabric

Add ¼" seam allowance around the outer edges of the design before cutting fabric

Cut the front and back muslin pieces for each potholder and the purse for them. Transfer the design onto the center of each front piece, embroider and tint each front piece.

For the purse, use ¼" seam allowance to sew the front to the back around the bottom edges, leaving the top edges between the marks on the pattern open. Fold back ¼" seam allowance along the edges of the top of the front piece. Fold the raw edge up under the seam allowance just a little. Whip stitch the folded edge in place across the wrong side. Repeat to finish the top edge of the back piece.

Layer the potholder front on top of the back piece, wrong sides facing. Using ¼" seam allowance, sew the front to the back, leaving a 1½" opening along one edge. Turn pieces to the right side. Insert the piece of batting into the potholder. Sew the opening closed. Make small randomly placed stitches through all layers to secure the batting layer in place.

As Simple as a Coloring Book

and as rewarding as a time-consuming masterpiece, tinted textiles hold a special place in the history of popular embroidery. Tuck-in toys, needle cases and even refrigerator bags once featured both tinted color and embroidery. Adding a touch of color transformed simple, popular motifs into timeless treasures.

Scotties

Quilt photo on page 99.
Patterns are shown 100%.

January

Hand Tinted Novelties

were such an accepted part of needlework catalogs that it is simply impossible to imagine the 1920's, 1930's and 1940's without them. Collectors today appreciate the charm and unique personality of tinted linens, yet their history remains largely untold. We do know that women used tinting to add color to their embroidery while following this trend.

evening

Continued on page 86.

February

From Colonial Silk Samplers

to Victorian crazy quilts, enhancing embroidery with painted color has been a part of popular embroidery since the late 18th century. In the 1890's, beautifully hand-colored pillow tops for elaborately shaded 'needlepainting' became the first commercially colored embroidery kits. Tinted novelty pillows featuring characters like Buster Brown or Dolly Dingle were popular as well.

Scotties

Quilt photo on page 99.
Patterns are shown 100%.

Following the Newest Fashions

in the home from Art Nouveau and Craftsman to Art Deco and Colonial Revivals, tinted pillows rapidly grew to be an essential part of any successful needlework catalog. Needlework magazines responded to their readers' interest in tinting at home with how-to articles and projects.

Continued on page 88.

During the 1920's

when prosperous homemakers were more interested in entertaining than elaborate needlework, a charmingly simple style of tinted linens appeared. Developed with a few colorful touches of thread or outlined with black running stitches, the color schemes and soft or flat shading perfectly suited America's modernized way of life.

it's eat

Scotties

Quilt photo on page 99.
Patterns are shown 100%.

May

Tinted Embroidery for the Nursery

rapidly emerged as the hottest craze for using the technique. Women discovered that another children's item, the wax crayon, allowed them to add their own color without the mess and trouble of oil paints and stencils.

and frolic

Continued on page 90.

June

Throughout the 1930's

when needlework of all kinds provided a lifeline of productive entertainment, embroidered novelties ranged from feminine confections to sporting motifs. Whimsical kitchen items were among the most noteworthy trends in tinted kits, cheering up everything from elaborate aprons to adorable potholders.

Scotties

Quilt photo on page 99.
Patterns are shown 100%.

Tinting Continued

as an essential coloring element in Victory novelties during the war, then it decorated the quilts and crib sheets, cuddling the first arrivals of the baby boom.

and play

Continued on page 92.

August

Tinted Novelties Disappeared

from catalogs so suddenly that it must have been a shock to customers. Perhaps the style didn't suit modern designers or the processes cost too much.

Scotties

Quilt photo on page 99.
Patterns are shown 100%.

September

Women Lost the Tradition

of using crayon and oil paints as they explored early textile paints, which proved to be rather heavy and opaque. This most charming, rewarding embroidery was, it seemed, completely extinguished except in fine silk painting.

be happy

Continued on page 94.

October

The Beauty of These Collectible Linens

is too enticing for today's creative stitcher to resist. With this generous collection of vintage samples to guide you, you can soon have a nursery, a kitchen or an entire home bursting with the color only tinting can provide, not to mention a heart brimming with pride over your accomplishments.

Scotties

Quilt photo on page 99.
Patterns are shown 100%.

Why Should You be Denied the Pleasure

of watching fluffy puppies and billowing hoop skirts materialize from a few splashes of color and dashes of thread? Because you can't paint? Because you had trouble coloring inside the lines? Piffle, ladies, piffle! Tinted linens are one of the oldest forms of popular needlework in existence. They have always been created by women.

and gay

December

Tinted Textile Timeline

1880 to Late 1890's - *Some commercial kits available.* • *Painted, embellished embroidery commonly suggested in fancywork columns in early 1880's.* • *First wax crayons are manufactured. Almost immediately, project ideas appear in fancywork columns suggesting using crayons to add color to embroidery.*

1890's - 1915 - *Kits handtinted for needlepainting color guides.* • *Some stitchers conserve silks and simply outline stitch around painted designs.* • *Realistic illustrations evolve into Craftsman motifs.* • *Tinted novelties include lodge pillows, penwipers, match strikers and photo frames. Strong interest in home tinting is evident.*

1920 - 1930 - *Tinting used with outline stitching for its own decorative quality.* • *Illustration styles show growing Art Deco influence.* • *Kits for soft dolls, bean bags, quilts and even play clothes are popular. Useful novelties such as tinted mending and laundry bags feature colonial ladies, mammies and large florals.* • *Crayon projects frequently appear in needlework columns.* • *Special textile paints, similar to silk paints, first available for home use.*

1930 - 1940 - *Airbrushing replaces hand stencilling in commercial kits. Soft flat colors echo the strong graphic style of period textiles. The late 1920's vogue for elaborately tinted hostess aprons continues, accompanied by elaborately tinted whimsical potholder sets. Colorful nursery projects almost replace 'plain' embroidery. Tinted 'boudoir' pillows and other decorative grown-up projects feature more sophisticated motifs. 'Crayon craft' patterns available from pattern services. Quilting columns frequently suggest using crayons to color applique blocks as an alternative to applique.*

1940 - 1950 - *Tinting survives the war as a decorative vogue.* • *California potteries bring bright, sophisticated yet casual themes into the home, strongly influencing tinted textile motifs.* • *'Victory' projects feature soldiers, planes and other military themes for every room in the house.* • *Among the most poignant tinted 'Victory' novelties are 'Gold-Star' samplers with the stars indicating sons lost in service.*

1954 - 1990's - *Tinted projects abruptly disappear from needlework catalogs and shops.* • *Crayon coloring on fabric is suggested primarily for children's crafts.* • *Colored, iron-on decals develop as a distinct category.* • *As baby boomers, tinted crib sheets are relegated to mothballs, they go unreplaced in the market.* • *The abundance of popular embroidery created between 1920 and 1950 is seemingly inexhaustible, limiting its price and collectibility.*

1995 to present - *On-line auctions and growing nostalgia market transform tinted linens into hot collectibles.* • *Prices for fine quality crib sheets surge from $20 to around $100.* • *Specialties such as Craftsman era or WWII memorabilia command even higher prices.* • *Fiber artists renewed interest in hand-coloring makes improved textile paints more widely available.* • *Crayon coloring is rediscovered by quilters as part of a growing interest in embroidered quilts.*

Embroidery Stitches

Working with Floss.
Separate embroidery floss.

Use 24" lengths of floss and a #8 embroidery needle.

Use 2 to 3 ply floss to outline large elements of the design and to embroider larger and more stylized patterns.

Use 2 ply for the small details on some items.

Blanket Stitch

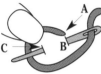

Come up at A, hold the thread down with your thumb, go down at B. Come back up at C with the needle tip over the thread. Pull the stitch into place. Repeat, outlining with the bottom legs of the stitch. Use this stitch to edge fabrics.

Chain Stitch

Come up at A. To form a loop, hold the thread down with your thumb, go down at B (as close as possible to A). Come back up at C with the needle tip over the thread. Repeat to form a chain.

Cross Stitch

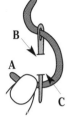

Make a diagonal Straight stitch (up at A, down at B) from upper right to lower left. Come up at C and go down at D to make another diagonal Straight stitch the same length as the first one. The stitch will form an X.

French Knot

Come up at A. Wrap the floss around the needle 2 to 3 times. Insert the needle close to A. Hold the floss and pull the needle through the loops gently.

Herringbone Stitch

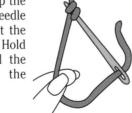

Come up at A. Make a slanted stitch to the top right, inserting the needle at B. Come up a short distance away at C.

Insert the needle at D to complete the stitch. Bring the needle back up at the next A to begin a new stitch. Repeat.

Pay attention to backgrounds.

When working with lighter-colored fabrics, do not carry dark flosses across large unworked background areas. Stop and start again to prevent unsightly 'ghost strings' from showing through the front.

Another option is to back tinted muslin with another layer of muslin before you add embroidery stitches. This will help keep 'ghost strings' from showing.

Lazy Daisy Stitch -

Come up at A. Go down at B (right next to A) to form a loop. Come back up at C with the needle tip over the thread. Go down at D to make a small anchor stitch over the top of the loop.

Running Stitch

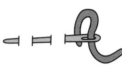

Come up at A. Weave the needle through the fabric, making short, even stitches. Use this stitch to gather fabrics, too.

Satin Stitch

Work small straight stitches close together and at the same angle to fill an area with stitches. Vary the length of the stitches as required to keep the outline of the area smooth.

Stem Stitch

Work from left to right to make regular, slanting stitches along the stitch line. Bring the needle up above the center of the last stitch. Also called 'Outline' stitch.

Straight Stitch

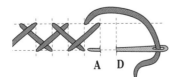

Come up at A and go down at B to form a simple flat stitch. Use this stitch for hair for animals and for simple petals on small flowers.

Whip Stitch

Insert the needle under a few fibers of one layer of fabric. Bring the needle up through the other layer of fabric. Use this stitch to attach the folded raw edges of fabric to the back of pieces or to attach bindings around the edges of quilts and coverlets.

Care of Linens

Washing -

- Test for colorfastness on the seam allowance. Let several drops of water fall through the fabric onto white blotter paper. If color appears, the fabric is not colorfast.
- To set dye, soak fabric in water and vinegar.
- Wash with a very mild detergent or soap, using tepid water. Follow all label instructions carefully.
- Do not use chlorine bleach on fine linen. Whiten it by hanging it in full sunlight.

Stain Removal -

- Grease - Use a presoak fabric treatment and wash in cold water.
- Nongreasy - Soak in cold water to neutralize the stain. Apply a presoak and then wash in cold water.
- Ballpoint Ink - Place on an absorbent material and soak with denatured or rubbing alcohol. Apply room temperature glycerin and flush with water. Finally, apply ammonia and quickly flush with water.
- Candle Wax - Place fabric between layers of absorbent paper and iron on low setting. Change paper as it absorbs wax. If a stain remains, wash with peroxide bleach.
- Rust - Remove with lemon juice, oxalic acid or hydrofluoric acid.

Storage -

- Wash and rinse thoroughly in soft water.
- Do not size or starch.
- Place cleaned linen on acid-free tissue paper and roll loosely.
- Line storage boxes with a layer of acid-free tissue paper.
- Place rolled linens in a box. Do not stack. Weight causes creases.
- Do not store linens in plastic bags.
- Hang linen clothing in a muslin bag or cover with a cotton sheet.

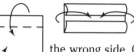

BOWTIE BLOCKS:

1. Use 1/4" seam allowances.
2. With right sides facing, stack sets of 2 assorted 5 1/4" Red squares together. Combine Light Red squares with Medium Red squares, as well as Light Red squares with Dark Red pieces, but also make a few Medium Red and Dark Red pairs. Stitch diagonally (corner to corner) to join each pair of squares.
3. Cut each set of squares in half across the other diagonal, perpendicular to the stitches.
4. Cut a 1/2" seam allowance on opposite edges of stitching on each piece. Lay matched triangle scraps aside.
5. Trim the seam allowance to 1/4". Press the seams open.
6. With right sides facing, match the seams and align raw edges of the 2 pressed triangles. Stitch triangles together to form squares. Press seams open. Square and trim each square to measure 4 3/4" on each side. Make 62 bowtie squares.

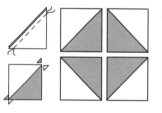

BOWTIE KNOTS:

Fold back 1/2" along each long side of each bowtie strip toward the center of the wrong side. Crease with finger or press with an iron. Fold back 1/2" along each end of each strip toward the center of the wrong side. Position the middle of the strip over the center of the square triangles on the bowtie squares. Using fusible seam tape, iron the strips in place.

CORNER SQUARES:

Sew each of the reserved small triangle pairs together to form a square. Press the seams open. Trim each square to measure 2 5/8". Make 80 small squares. Sew 4 of the small squares together into a corner block. Press seams. Square each block and cut to measure 4 3/4".

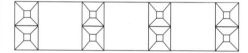

ASSEMBLY:

1. Use 1/4" seam allowances throughout.
2. With right sides facing, sew a corner square to a bowtie square, add another bowtie square. Repeat twice more to alternate a corner square with 2 bowtie squares across a row. End with a corner square. Repeat to make 5 rows. Press the seams open.

3. Sew 2 bowtie squares together, one on top of the other. Repeat to make 16 stacked bowtie blocks. Alternate 4 stacked blocks with 3 White squares to make 4 rows. Press the seams toward the stacked blocks.
4. With right sides facing, sew rows together as shown on page 99. Press the seams toward the narrower rows.
5. With right sides facing, sew the 2 backing pieces together down the center long edge. Press the seam open.
6. Layer the backing batting and the assembled top to form a sandwich. Baste the layers together. Quilt as desired.
7. Remove the basting stitches. Trim the backing and batting even with the edges of the quilt top.
8. Bind edges with the Red strips.